WHY
WOMEN
CAN'T
SLEEP

Women's new mental implosion

BY

MELVIS MICHAEL

Table of content

Chapter five

Gen X ladies need to at the same time focus on small kids and old guardians - with little help.

Chapter six

Gen X ladies can battle to track down that ideal accomplice or have kids when they're prepared.

Chapter seven

Everybody recognizes that teens go through a tremendous physiological change during adolescence. Perimenopause is a likewise tremendous hormonal commotion that influences ladies in middle age.

Chapter eight

Come to harmony with your emotional meltdown by getting genuine.

Significant guidance

INTRODUCTION

. These ladies were sold the story that nothing was preventing them from accomplishing their most out of this world fantasies, when actually they've confronted gigantic difficulties to excel. Besides the fact that they graduated into a terrible work market, they likewise face orientation and age separation and time and again wind up focusing on small kids and old guardians all the while. All that they've accomplished has been against gigantic chances.

Presentation

How might this benefit me? Find the untold story of ladies' emotional meltdowns.

At this point, we've all become exceptionally used to the figure of speech of the male emotional meltdown. The cliché man will awaken one day profoundly unsatisfied with his life. He'll purchase a yellow Ferrari, grow a facial hair growth, or take up riding in Hawaii as a leisure activity. Or on the other hand, obviously, he'll leave his better half for a lot more youthful lady.

Not minding how it is, does it mean something shouldn't have been said about the ladies? Ladies are portrayed as responding to these emergencies, obviously, they have their own. This is maybe most genuine for ladies of Generation X, who were brought into the world somewhere in the range of 1965 and 1980 - a period of extraordinary monetary and political flimsiness. These ladies were guaranteed that they could accomplish everything: an effective vocation as well as a flourishing family and public activity.

Reeling under the heaviness of these assumptions, Gen X ladies are in the pains of a serious existential emergency as they arrive at middle-age. They are restless and angry, and they lay there restlessly around evening time. In any case, this is normally difficult to see from an external perspective, as they rarely obliterate their relationships or purchase vehicles in shocking varieties.

In these squints, you'll get an image of what emotional meltdown truly resembles for ladies, what causes it, and what sort of help ladies truly need.

In these squints, you'll find

why obligation is weakening Gen X's arrangements for progress;the additional obligations that fall on Gen X ladies;andhow tolerating that life is a struggle can really be enabling.

Chapter one

Age X ladies were informed they could accomplish anything - yet the fantasy didn't compare reality.

Each young lady who experienced childhood in America during the 1980s knows all about the Enjoli fragrance promotion. It showed an unquenchably vigorous blonde lady trading a savvy matching suit for some enjoyable garments while she prepares supper for her family, then progressing into a femme fatale in a semi-formal dress ready to lure her better half. Also, she appeared to hold her light energy all through!

This promotion embodies the fantasy about "having everything" that American ladies naturally introduced to Generation X grew up with, a commitment that ladies can do and be anything. They didn't need to be attendants; they could be specialists all things considered. They didn't need to make due with being a secretary when they could be the CEO.

This commitment was immensely energizing, and showed the advancement of second-wave women's activists. These ladies accomplished wins like passing the government regulation Title IX in 1972, which declared that young ladies could never again be oppressed in governmentally subsidized instructive projects.

Yet, these additional opportunities likewise accompanied gigantic strain. The commitment that young ladies could do everything transformed into an objective. Young ladies should do everything. Now that ladies had these opportunities, there was hypothetically nothing halting them accomplishing their fantasies with the exception of an absence of creative mind or reluctance to invest the effort.

Notwithstanding, ladies naturally introduced to Generation X have confronted primary hindrances to accomplishing their aspirations that don't have anything to do with their singular characteristics or drive. For a certain something, they grew up through progressive downturns which caused monetary precarity and occupation weakness, implying that ladies who experienced childhood in this age are frequently burdened with colossal measures of obligation. For something else, orientation jobs haven't changed to reflect additional opportunities that ladies have in the work environment.

Saying that ladies are allowed to do anything while at the same time disregarding the huge difficulties they face makes unreasonable assumptions. It likewise makes a culture of disgrace. Numerous ladies brought up in this time have assimilated the account that their lives are brimming with vast conceivable outcomes. They fault themselves when they can't accomplish all that they'd expected, significantly less satisfy the Enjoli aroma good example they grew up with.

Chapter two

Gen X ladies face both orientation and age segregation in the work environment.

Assuming Facebook Chief Operating Officer, Sheryl Sandberg is to be accepted, each lady can find actual success in the working environment in the event that they simply incline in and request that they're genuinely redressed and advanced. So for what reason do so many Gen X ladies wind up in unsafe or low-paying position in their middle age?

Ladies who were raised accepting that the CEO's office was theirs for the taking have been extremely frustrated to confront gigantic measures of orientation separation. This is in spite of the multitude of hard-won women's activist additions of the Boomer age. As a matter of fact, by mid-vocation, men are 70% more probable than ladies to have senior leader positions. By late profession that distinction broadens to a tremendous 142%.

In any event, when ladies truly do have a similar work title, they frequently procure significantly not exactly their male partners. While the compensation hole among people is by all accounts diminishing, with ladies procuring 82 pennies to each male dollar in 2017, the image turns out to be a lot starker on the off chance that you see moderately aged ladies. By 40 years of age, ladies just procure 73 pennies to the male dollar. What's more, in the event that you investigate the range of a 15-year profession, considering periods where ladies are compelled to get some much needed rest work, their compensation drops to just 49 pennies to the dollar.

Gen X ladies face a one-two punch of orientation, yet in addition age segregation. They're compelled to rival Millennials who are seen by businesses as being more insightful at occupations including the web and virtual entertainment. An examination by the New York Times uncovered that age segregation is even incorporated into how some Facebook work advertisements are disseminated; broadcast communications organization Verizon, for instance, as of late determined that main long term olds ought to have their work promotions appearing in their channels.

The preliminaries of the gig market lead numerous Gen X ladies to go to outsourcing. This work is frequently introduced as engaging, an opportunity to "get compensated living life to the fullest." But it accompanies numerous stressors, similar to a conflicting pay, inconsistent work hours, and all the organization and bother of maintaining your own business.

Uncontrolled separation has made it undeniably challenging for Gen X ladies to excel. Regardless of good degrees, steadiness, and each readiness to "incline in," steady and well-paying position keep on evading them. As we'll find in the following squint, experiencing childhood in exceptionally unsafe monetary times has just made it harder.

Chapter three

The desires of Gen X ladies are foiled by piles of obligation.

The Boomer age lived in a universe of practically staggering monetary thriving and steadiness by the present norms. A working class family in America could reside serenely on one pay, own their own home, and work at similar organization for their entire lives.

That image presently appears as rosily hopeful as a fantasy. Gen X is impressively less fortunate than their folks, without any expectation of making up lost ground. The 1987 financial exchange crash provoked a downturn similarly as more established Gen Xers were getting ready to enter the work environment. In 1993, the time-based compensation hit an extraordinary failure, implying that individuals began their professions in a tough spot.

Then, at that point, similarly as Gen X ladies were attempting to make strides in their vocations, the dotcom bubble burst in 2001, provoking another financial exchange crash and downturn. The Bureau of Labor Statistics reports that 2.7 million positions were lost somewhere in the range of 2001 and 2002 alone!

One thing Gen X ladies could get was a home credit, as home loans were exceptionally simple to obtain in the mid 2000s. While at long last possessing property appeared to them like a little glimpse of heaven, the fantasy transformed into a bad dream in 2007, with the subprime contract emergency and breakdown of the lodging bubble. The houses they had quite recently purchased lost up to 30% of their worth practically short-term.

Obviously, today Gen X has a stunning measure of obligation - 82% more than Boomers and $37,000 more than the public normal. Be that as it may, this obligation isn't all because of the downturns. Gen Xers likewise convey devastating understudy loans, because of the expanding cost of advanced education, and are in many cases in the red for costs connected with medical services. An absence of steady employments brings about an absence of admittance to medical coverage. That implies that one wellbeing alarm can dive a family into monetary emergency.

While all Gen Xers face these conditions, there is likewise a gendered aspect to obligation: besides the fact that men normally land the great positions, ladies are typically likewise troubled with the largest part of costs connected with childcare, in instances of separation, and really focusing on weak guardians.

Adapting to this huge obligation implies that ladies have frequently needed to require profession intends to be postponed, or leave their innovative aspirations to acknowledge any work they can find that helps cover their bills.

Chapter four

Despite the fact that Gen X ladies are more present in the working environment, they currently give substantially more opportunity to childcare.

It's astounding how much normal insight about nurturing can move in only one age. The creator recalls long evenings spent sitting in front of the TV in an unfilled house while her folks were working, and meandering the roads openly with her companions. Her folks took care of and dressed her and gave her sanctuary, yet not much else.

Today, nurturing appears to have become a great deal more confounded. Working class guardians are supposed to effectively animate their kids' minds, connect with them in imaginative play, make them home-prepared feasts, and genuinely focus on them.

In an undeniably cutthroat school system, kids' schoolwork currently must be effectively administered to guarantee they are fruitful and can submit serious applications to colleges.

Also, in the midst of worries about security, kids are not generally permitted to wander the roads uninhibitedly. All things considered, they're transported from one coordinated wearing or social action to another.

These exercises are massively tedious, and the main part of this work is as yet embraced by moms - on top of longer hours at work.

 As a matter of fact, a Pew Research Center review shows that moms currently give 25 hours of the week to paid work, contrasted with their 1965 ancestors' 9 hours out of each week. They additionally do a normal of 14 week after week long stretches of childcare, in contrast with the past age's 10. Conversely, men do a normal of 8 hours of childcare consistently. This is multiple times what their 1965 ancestors did, yet way beneath what ladies do.

However, these figures don't cover the work ladies do in the house that can't be measured, which is called imperceptible work. Generally, the ladies of the family will make sure to purchase a birthday card for a grandparent, get an instructor's finish of-term present, plan regular checkups, answer school messages, and make sure to purchase new socks. Basically, ladies are entrusted with intellectually dealing with the family notwithstanding all of their work liabilities. They convey a tremendous, imperceptible mental burden.

Also, Gen X womens' caretaking obligations don't end with their family units. As we'll hear in the following squint, that is just the start.

Chapter five

Gen X ladies need to at the same time focus on small kids and old guardians - with little help.

Envision you're wrestling with the tremendous requests of really focusing on two little youngsters simultaneously as adjusting a task and attempting to keep the house all together. Similarly as your most youthful youngster begins school and you're carving out a smidgen greater opportunity for yourself, one of your folks has a wellbeing emergency. Abruptly, you really want to begin supporting them as well.

This is the experience of numerous Gen X ladies. As they're having kids later, in their 30s and even 40s, they frequently wind up managing the gigantic requests of childcare simultaneously as their folks are developing slight and coming to rely upon them. Similarly as with childcare, ladies are lumped with a large portion of crafted by dealing with older guardians. Those guardians are frequently separated and don't have support from each other, compounding the weight.

This huge obligation of being the principal carer for small kids and guardians all the while is just made more diligently by the way that encouraging groups of people have dwindled. Today, it's become more uncommon for neighbors and childless companions to assist with childcare. What's more, on the grounds that the Boomer age had less youngsters, Gen Xers thusly frequently have less kin to assist with alleviating the burden.

 While strict networks used to be a backbone of help in upsetting times, as the Gen X age has become less strict, they are in many cases less engaged with those networks and every one of the assets that they used to give.

On the off chance that you live in the United States, you will not have the option to rely upon the public authority for much assistance all things considered. There is a regulation that representatives can go home for the weeks work for maternity leave or other family concerns, yet those weeks are neglected, and the law just covers 60% of American laborers at any rate. The rest falls beyond it, and can be immediately terminated for getting some much needed rest for family or wellbeing reasons.

It doesn't take a ton of creative mind to comprehend that these providing care requests, combined with an absence of cultural help, make colossal measures of pressure for the ladies of Gen X, the "sandwich age," who are extended very slight.

Chapter six

Gen X ladies can battle to track down that ideal accomplice or have kids when they're prepared.

The present discussion about the difficulty of being a mother could make you ponder dumping the entire thing all together.

Some Gen X ladies have for sure pursued the decision not to have youngsters, rather focusing on different connections, work, travel, and everything that guardians lack the capacity to deal with. This development is called Childfree by Choice. Yet, it is altogether different to being somebody who needed to have kids however couldn't.

Tragically, some Gen X ladies fit into this last option camp of ladies. Why?

Here and there this is on the grounds that they couldn't find an accomplice they needed to begin a family with. While the lighthearted comedies we grew up with gave us the feeling that affection is in every case not far off, it tends to be extremely slippery for sure.

As a matter of fact, in the event that you're a hetero lady searching for a man in New York City, you're now in a tough spot, as there are 400,000 additional ladies than men. You'd imagine that cutting edge dating applications like Tinder would help, yet some accept that innovation makes things harder, working with a culture where individuals are continually swiping and searching for something better.

A few ladies have at long last tracked down the ideal accomplice or chose to attempt to bring up a kid alone, yet find they can't consider or convey a child to term. This is incompletely on the grounds that ladies are presently attempting to have kids later than any past age.

This is empowered to some extent by advancements like IVF, spearheaded in 1978, or egg freezing, which previously prompted an effective birth in 1999. While these advances have broadened richness for certain ladies, they don't necessarily in every case work. In 2016, just 22% of IVF techniques were fruitful.

The strain to explore the dating scene and pursue a choice on when to begin attempting to have a child can be extraordinarily upsetting for Gen X ladies. On paper, we have such countless options. Yet, by and by, there are unassailable hindrances, as never meeting the co-parent of your fantasies or figuring out that you're not ready to imagine a youngster.

Hormonal changes can affect ladies in middle age, however clinical help is deficient.

As of late as 1970, an individual from the Democratic Party's Committee on National Priorities contended that battling for orientation uniformity wasn't fundamentally important. His explanation? Ladies' chemicals were so hazardous to their thinking skills they would never be endowed with high-positioning positions. He contended that ladies couldn't be pilots or presidents or CEOs in light of the fact that their chemicals would "imperil the world."

In light of unmitigated sexism like this, women's activists battling for uniformity declared that ladies could work precisely too as men can. That, obviously, is valid - ladies can be similarly as powerful at any particular employment.

However, cis ladies in all actuality do vary physiologically from cis men. We have remarkable chemicals, which influence our lives in unambiguous ways. Being compelled to reject that for such a long time in the battle for fairness meaningfully affects moderately aged ladies' wellbeing and prosperity.

Chapter seven

Everybody recognizes that teens go through a tremendous physiological change during adolescence. Perimenopause is a likewise tremendous hormonal commotion that influences ladies in middle age. While most ladies go through menopause at age 51, the hormonal movements start a whole lot sooner - close to a decade prior for African-American ladies and seven years before for white ladies. So currently in their forties ladies can encounter weakening hot blazes, as well as restlessness, difficult sex, a low charisma, bosom torment, and diminished hunger. They can likewise encounter bewildering emotional episodes and serious sensations of uneasiness and fury. There are successful medicines, similar to chemical substitution treatment, which can radically diminish these side effects. Yet, numerous ladies don't have the foggiest idea what's the deal with them, quit worrying about how to treat it. As a matter of fact, 42% of ladies have never at any point examined menopause with their wellbeing suppliers. Furthermore, as a general rule, specialists themselves are oblivious: as per a 2013 study at Johns Hopkins, just a single in five obstetrics and gynecology occupants are given conventional preparation about menopause. Gen X ladies, as we've seen, are as of now under a huge measure of pressure. What's more, going through the significant physiological changes brought about by menopause without great clinical or social help just aggravates it.

Chapter eight

Come to harmony with your emotional meltdown by getting genuine.

We've all become acquainted with broadcasting artificially glamorized pictures of the best version of ourselves via web-based entertainment. Seeing these can lead us to accept that others lead much better, more monetarily dissolvable, or more intriguing lives than we do.In any case, truly, by far most of moderately aged ladies are under a huge measure of pressure. Recognizing that, to ourselves and to one another, can break the disconnection of the emergency.

Understanding that a considerable lot of the assumptions you grew up with are ridiculous will assist with night more. Gen X ladies were raised to accept they could do and have everything. However, there are significant obstructions to a fruitful profession, reserve funds in the bank, and a simple home life that are all the way beyond our control.

Conceding that could sound pessimist, however as a matter of fact, it tends to very engage. It implies that all that we have accomplished has been won against gigantic chances. What's more, it likewise implies that we're not insane for feeling anxious. Our lives can be truly hard. Feeling tense, restless, or discouraged accordingly is an extremely fitting response.

Looking for help is the following significant stage. This can be from companions or similar ladies who are in a comparable situation; a decent specialist; or a specialist who really is familiar with how to help perimenopausal ladies. It can appear as a canine walker, a bookkeeper, or a relative who wouldn't fret doing some looking after children. Requesting assist with canning be hard when you've been raised to attempt to be totally independent. In any case, it's so significant.

It might feel like this period of your life will continue perpetually - that you'll continuously be extended flimsy between the entirety of your obligations, that you'll constantly have a so pitiable outlook on your vocation. Yet, the excellence of a stage is that it closes. You won't be moderately aged until the end of time. Your children will grow up, your chemicals will quiet down, and you'll get to encounter a period of life that numerous ladies track down significantly more satisfying and fascinating.

So past changing your assumptions and requesting help, one of the most mind-blowing ways of overcoming an emotional meltdown is basically to pause and recollect that it will pass.

The vital message in these flickers:

Gen X ladies grew up being informed that the world was their clam and they could satisfy their women's activist all progenitors' dreams: an incredible work, an equivalent division of homegrown work, and an opportunity to affect the world. In any case, the fact of the matter is very unique. Gen X ladies have experienced childhood in unsafe monetary times, with devastating obligation and the overwhelming majority of providing care liabilities. This makes a tension cooker of stress and unfulfilled assumptions, prompting an emotional meltdown. Yet, help is accessible, and eventually the emergency will pass.

Significant guidance:

Make your own general public or club.
One of the most incredible ways of interfacing with similar individuals - whatever your ongoing life circumstance - is to set up a month to month meeting around a common interest. For instance, you could have a margarita-drinking club, a journalists' general public, or a month to month seedling trade. Having that ordinary contact will be an extraordinary method for getting backing and break your feeling of disconnection.
About the Author

About the Author

MELVIS MICHAEL is a researcher and a writer. She's authored "ebook writing and Publishing made easy" and "bathing bombs". She also has many books that'll soon be published. She's also a pharmacist by profession.